Little Tom Tucker,
He sang for his supper.
What did he sing for?
Why, white bread and butter.
How can I cut it without a knife?
How can I marry without a wife?

Designed by Ivor Claydon and Bob Hook.
Cover design by J. C. Suarès.
Illustrations researched and chosen by Karin B. Hills,
with grateful thanks to the Colin Mears Collection.
Produced by Sheldrake Press Ltd., 188 Cavendish Road,
London SW12 0DA, England.

ISBN 0-941434-88-5

Published in the U.S.A. in 1986 by
Stewart, Tabori & Chang, Inc., 740 Broadway,
New York, New York 10003

Distributed by Workman Publishing
1 West 39 Street, New York, New York 10018

Typesetting by Rowland Phototypesetting (London) Ltd.
Printed and bound in England by W.S. Cowell Limited, Butter Market, Ipswich.

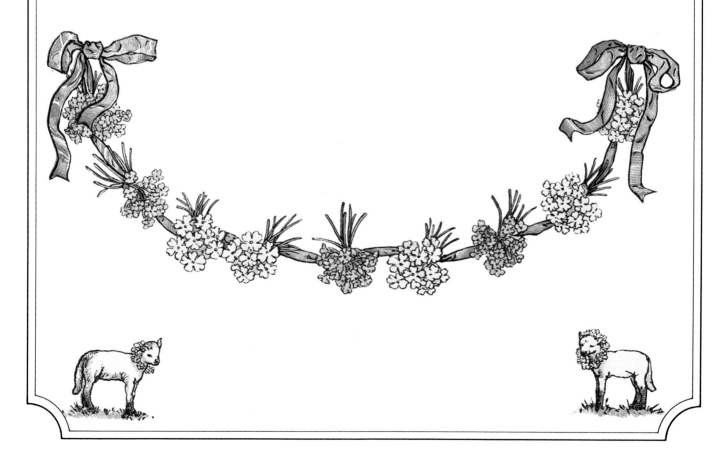

THE KATE GREENAWAY

BABY BOOK

STEWART, TABORI & CHANG
NEW YORK

KATE GREENAWAY, the doyenne of nursery writers and illustrators, was born in London in 1846. Her father, John Greenaway, was a draftsman and wood engraver working mainly for *The Illustrated London News*. Kate's greatest delight as a small girl was to creep downstairs while the rest of the family slept, to watch him labor through the night on an urgent engraving for the magazine. Recognizing that she had a passion for drawing, her parents sent her at the early age of twelve to the National Art Training School, now the Royal College of Art, in London.

In 1868 she had a watercolor and six small drawings accepted for exhibition by the Dudley Gallery in Piccadilly, which in turn led to varied commissions for greetings cards, calendars, and book and magazine illustrations. In 1877 came the turning point in her career, when she met the forward-thinking engraver and printer Edmund Evans and presented him with a collection of her own rhymes and pictures entitled *Under the Window*. Evans loved it at once, and had the conviction and courage to print a first edition of 20,000 copies. It sold out before he could reprint. For more than a decade thereafter the partnership flourished, producing such classics of children's literature as *Marigold Garden, Mother Goose, A Day in a Child's Life, A Apple Pie,* and *Language of Flowers.*

Kate Greenaway died in 1901. Though she never had sons and daughters of her own, children remained her passion for life. "No one has given us such clear-eyed, soft-faced, happy-hearted childhood," wrote the poet Austin Dobson, "or so poetically apprehended the coy reticences, the simplicities, and the small solemnities of little people." With their charmingly adapted end-of-the-eighteenth-century breeches, bonnets, smocks, and frocks, the open-faced children in her illustrations reminded her readers of the true values of innocence, joy, and beauty. They have lost none of their appeal or relevance today.

CONTENTS

THE BIRTH

Name———————————————— Time————————————————

Date———————————————— Place————————————————

Doctor———————————————— Name tag

Midwife/nurse————————————

Newspaper announcement

Weight_____   Color of hair_____

Length_____   Lock of hair

Color of eyes_____

Resemblances_____   Personality_____

_____   _____

_____   _____

_____   _____

_____   _____

_____   _____

_____   _____

_____   _____

First visitors _____

_____

_____

_____

_____

_____

_____

_____

_____

_____

_____

Gifts_____

_____

_____

_____

_____

_____

_____

_____

_____

_____

_____

_____

Cards_____

_____

_____

_____

_____

_____

_____

_____

_____

_____

_____

_____

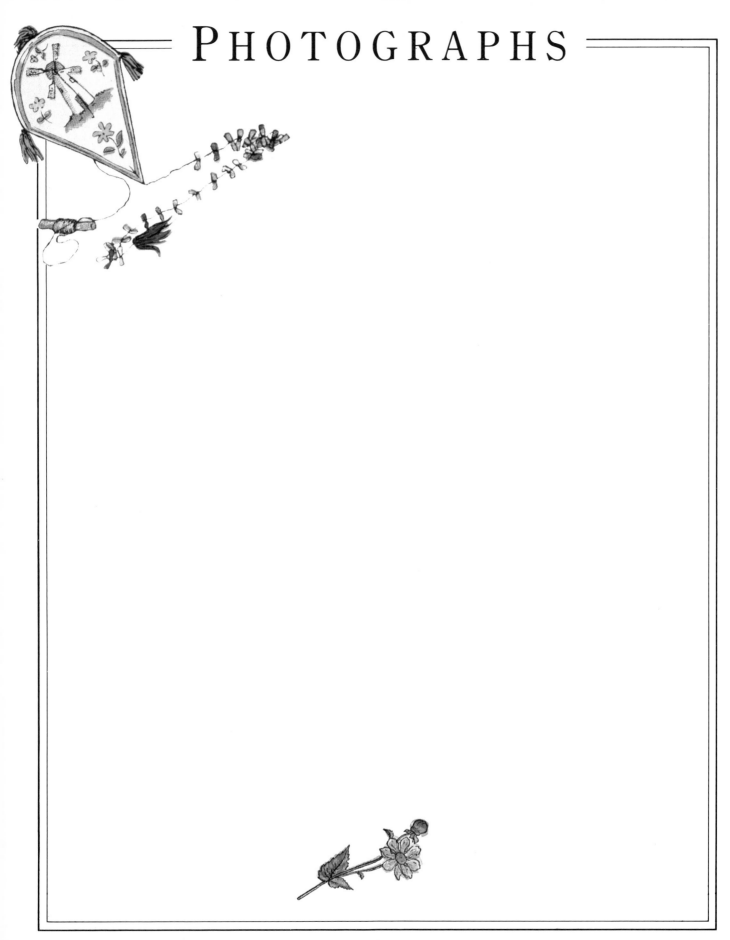

PHOTOGRAPHS

THE FAMILY TREE

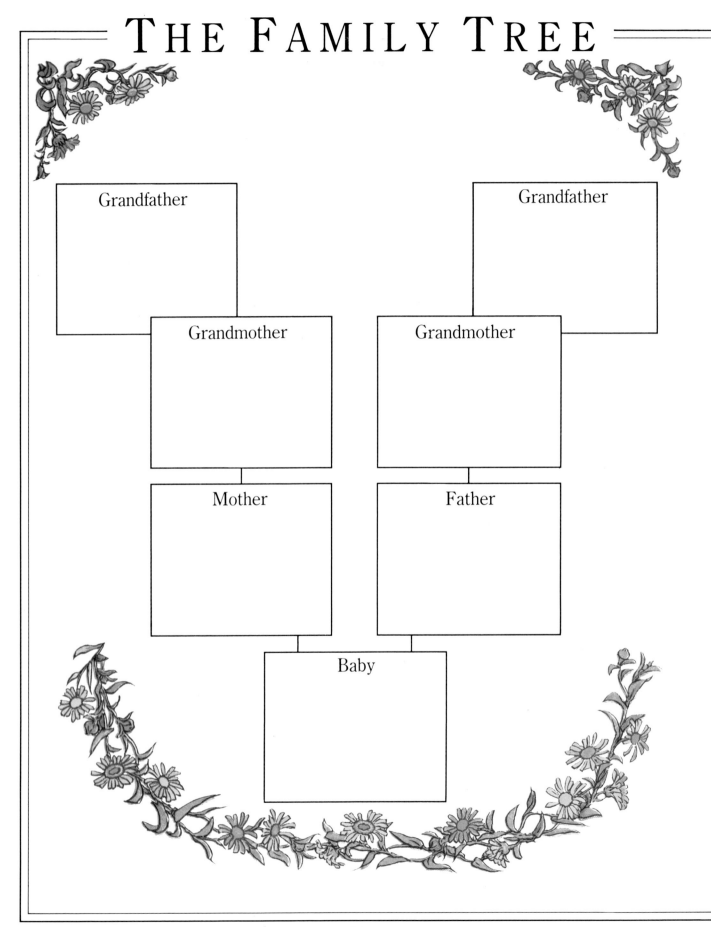

Grandfather

Grandfather

Grandmother

Grandmother

Mother

Father

Baby

Brothers and Sisters

_____

_____

_____

_____

_____

NAMING

Full name _____

_____

Date _____

Place _____

_____

Guests _____

_____

_____

_____

_____

_____

_____

_____

_____

Gifts _____

_____

_____

_____

_____

_____

_____

_____

_____

_____

PHOTOGRAPHS

Weight_____ _____

Length_____ _____

General progress_____ _____

_____ _____

_____ _____

_____ _____

_____ _____

_____ _____

_____ _____

PHOTOGRAPHS

WEIGHT

lbs

64

56

48

40

32

24

16

8

0   3 mos   6 mos   9 mos   1   1½   2   2½   3   3½   4   4½   5

AGE (months and years)

HEIGHT

ins

40

35

30

25

20

15

10

5

0   3   6   9   1   1½   2   2½   3   3½   4   4½
     mos   mos   mos

AGE (months and years)

VACCINATIONS

_____   _____

_____   _____

_____   _____

_____   _____

_____   _____

ILLNESSES

_____
_____
_____
_____
_____
_____
_____

AT SIX MONTHS

Weight _____ _____

Length _____ _____

General progress _____ _____

_____ _____

_____ _____

_____ _____

_____ _____

_____ _____

_____ _____

_____ _____

PHOTOGRAPHS

TEETH

Date   Upper

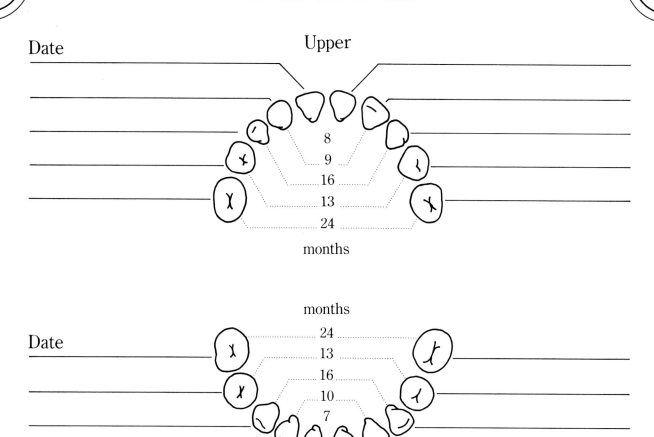

8
9
16
13
24

months

months
24
13
16
10
7

Date

Lower

FIRST WORDS

MILESTONES

Smiles _____

Sits _____

_____

_____

Laughs _____

Crawls _____

_____

_____

_____

_____

Stands_____

_____

_____

Walks_____

_____

_____

Spring.

Autumn.

Winter.

AT ONE YEAR

Weight_____

Height_____

General progress_____

_____

_____

_____

_____

_____

PHOTOGRAPHS

FIRST BIRTHDAY

AT TWO YEARS

FUNNY SAYINGS

_____

_____

_____

_____

_____

_____

_____

_____

_____

FAVORITES

Stories _____

_____

_____

_____

_____

_____

_____

_____

_____

Books _____

_____

_____

_____

_____

_____

Toys_____ Pets_____

_____ _____

_____ _____

_____ _____

_____ _____

_____ _____

_____ _____

_____ _____

Rhymes/poems _____

Games _____

_____

_____

_____

_____

_____

_____

_____

_____

_____

_____

_____

_____

_____

_____

Songs/lullabies_____

_____

_____

_____

Special interests_____

_____

_____

FIRST DRAWING

FIRST WRITING

GOING TO SCHOOL

Place_____

_____

Date_____

Teachers_____

_____

_____

_____

_____

Favorite activities_____

_____

_____

_____

_____

_____

_____

_____

_____

_____

_____

_____

_____

_____

_____

Special friends _____

_____

_____

_____

_____

_____

_____

Little Miss Muffet,
Sat on a tuffet,
Eating some curds and whey;
There came a great spider,
And sat down beside her,
And frightened Miss Muffet away.